Heronymus Heron Discovers His Shadow
(and a Whole Lot More)
By Janice Williams and Richard Skaare

Acknowledgments

We dedicate this book to our grandchildren: Zack, Gabby, Bella, Brooklyn, and Stella.

Our special thanks to our creative consultant and graphic designer, Ron MacDonald of Step2 Branding and Design, for bringing our vision to life with your engaging energy, your thoughtful input, and your outstanding design work.

Our thanks to our spouses, Dave Sandmann and Jane Skaare, for your encouragement and support in so many ways.

And to all those who have read and critiqued and listened to our endless stories about the writing, photography, and the birthing of this book, we are most grateful.

Finally, thanks to Heronymus for allowing Jan to photograph him and us to share his story.

THE CREATORS

Jan Williams

An avid wildlife photographer, Jan fell in love with a great blue heron she named Heronymus and, with her camera, captured his best angles and his shadows. With her four grandchildren in mind, she recruited talented storyteller Richard Skaare and, together, they visualized and wrote a tale that stirs the imagination and inspires heroism among readers and listeners.

Hero the Heron

Known to the locals as Henry and as Heronymus to others, Hero lives on the beach on Anna Maria Island, Florida. He is an accomplished fisherman, a popular attraction for tourists, and, until recently, a keep-to-himself bird. To all the other shorebirds — and to Jan and Richard — he is a dancer and a hero.

Richard Skaare

Richard spent his career as a corporate communicator and his life listening to and telling stories. A worldwide traveler, avocational writer and photographer, and a grandfather, Richard was taken by Jan Williams' photos of Heronymus Heron and joined her to create the fun story of a bird who realized that being different does not stop you from becoming a hero.

Copyright © 2020 Janice A. Williams and Richard Skaare. Photography by Janice A. Williams. All rights reserved.

No part of this book may be reproduced in any manner without the authors' expressed written consent, except in the case of brief excerpts in critical reviews and articles. Inquires about the book should be addressed to:

Jan Williams
Jan@HeroTheHeron.com
603-777-7004

Richard Skaare
Rich@HeroTheHeron.com
717-877-5180

ISBN:
Paperback: 978-1-950381-90-6
Hardcover: 978-1-950381-99-9
Library of Congress Control Number: 2020917695

Published by:
Piscataqua Press
32 Daniel St., Portsmouth, NH 03801
info@piscataquapress.com

HeroTheHeron.com

Heronymus Heron Discovers His Shadow
(and a Whole Lot More)

By Janice Williams and Richard Skaare

Heronymus Heron remembers when he first saw it.

He remembers **exactly** where he was.

He remembers **everything** about that Tuesday.

He was standing very still on the beach warming his feathers, looking out at the ocean, and thinking about his name.

2

Heronymus was a big name that was difficult to say...

HER-ON-E-MUSS...

and even harder to spell.

It made him feel different.

He was also a big bird, a Great Blue Heron to be exact, which made him **taller** and *different* than other birds.

Heronymus the Great Blue Heron sounded important, but he didn't think he was important.

In fact, feeling different and unimportant made him want to keep to himself.

But all that was about to change.

On that Tuesday, Heronymus did the same things he did every day.

In the morning, he flew from the tree where he sleeps to the beach beside the ocean.

He stood quietly in the shallow water, watching and waiting for some small curious fish to tickle his toes.

When a fish swam by, he dipped his long beak into the water and caught the fish.

Then he flipped the fish into his mouth, tipped his head back, and swallowed it down...

... no chewing, just one loooong GULP!

After that bit of breakfast, Heronymus walked the beach.

All the fishermen come to the beach in the morning with their long fishing poles, their bait boxes, and their fish pails.

Heronymus was looking for John because John shared the fish he caught and that made Heronymus feel special.

John was in his usual spot with his fishing line in the water.

Heronymus crept close to him, just a little bit at a time. Then he stood very still. He watched the fishing line and waited for John to catch a fish.

If the fish was too small to take home to eat, John would toss it to Heronymus.

If Heronymus got bored waiting for John to catch something, he tiptoed along the beach and tried to get his bill inside a fish pail. It was kind of like trying to sneak a cookie before dinner.

In the afternoon, the fishermen packed up their rods and pails and went home.

Heronymus was disappointed when John left the beach.

He cleaned his feathers, then stood alone looking straight ahead at the ocean.

Except when he was fishing, Heronymus rarely looked down. But on that afternoon, for the first time in a long time, he looked down at the sand,

and there it was!

Beside him on the beach was a dark gray flat bird.

And the dark gray flat bird was **alive!**

When Heronymus moved, it moved. Heronymus tried to ignore it, but whenever he looked over at it, it looked back at him.

He tried to turn his head quickly to see the flat bird without it seeing him. That didn't work.

At first, Heronymus did not like this different bird so close to him. Then he noticed that when he lifted his foot, the flat gray bird lifted his foot too.

That made Heronymus laugh. Heronymus could not remember the last time he laughed. But this little guy was really funny.

Just then Rosie the Royal Tern flew over to see why Heronymus was laughing. "Hey, look. You have a flat gray bird too!" Heronymus said to Rosie.

Hey, look. You have a flat gray bird too!

Rosie looked down. "Flat gray bird?" she said. "That's your shadow! Everyone has a shadow on sunny days. You simply have to look down to see it. Your shadow shows up whenever your body keeps the sun from hitting the ground.

Your shadow is your shape, so everyone's shadow is different."

Everyone's shadow is different!

Heronymus kept watching his new flat gray bird friend.

"Hello Shadow!" Heronymus said.

He began turning around in a circle, bobbing his head up and down, and moving his feet. Everything he did, his shadow did with him.

Hello, Shadow!

Heronymus and his shadow moved left together and then shuffled right. They dipped their tails down then up, wiggled their hips, stretched out their necks and pulled them back in.

Heronymus was dancing. He had never danced before!

He had to stop. He was out of breath. But dancing was so much fun! It was then that he noticed a lot of different birds gathered nearby, watching him.

Heronymus felt a little embarrassed, but he saw the other birds doing just what he had done, looking down and seeing their own dark gray birds, small and flat. When they moved, their shadows moved.

Cora the Cormorant called over to Heronymus, "Hey, let's get everyone dancing with their shadows, You start, Heronymus."

Heronymus noticed that he was the center of attention. That had never happened before. He was hesitant at first but then he decided to be brave and started moving his feet again and dancing.

"Hey, let's get everyone dancing!"

One by one, the birds joined in. The terns started first, lifting their wings, dipping their heads, and shaking their feathers as if they heard music.

Roy the Reddish Egret started his dance in the water. Amanda the American Oystercatcher began to prance, and a bunch of sandpipers started parading up the beach.

All the birds were having fun together!

"You're our hero!" said Rosie the Royal Tern. "You brought us together and taught us to dance. We should call you Hero rather than Heronymus."

Everyone agreed.

Even though he didn't think of himself as a hero, Heronymus liked his new name...

and...

being different didn't seem to matter now.

You're our hero!

The birds danced and cackled until the sun went down. And that was when Heronymus noticed that the flat gray birds disappeared.

The sun was gone and so were the shadows. But what a good time they had shared.

Everyone knew that they had never been this happy.

"Who knows," Hero said.
"Maybe we could do this again.
Let's all come back here and dance tomorrow!
Same time, same place.

Maybe we could do this again!

If the flat gray birds don't show up, we will just pretend they are here and have another dance party."

And so they did.

Every day after that Tuesday, Hero made sure he looked down a lot. Sometimes his shadow was there, sometimes not.

But,

Hero was happy that he had new friends.

He was happy that it was okay to be different.

And he was happy that he was the only dancing Great Blue Heron on the beach.

Jan Williams and Richard Skaare
High school friends, professional communicators, grandparents and bird-lovers — they blended their talents in photography and storytelling to create this delightful and engaging book about an everyday character who speaks to the hero in each of us.

www.ingramcontent.com/pod-product-compliance
Lightning Source LLC
Chambersburg PA
CBHW041800290426
43661CB00132B/1227